Anonymous

The Rindge Gifts to the City of Cambridge, Massachusetts

Anonymous

The Rindge Gifts to the City of Cambridge, Massachusetts

ISBN/EAN: 9783744670807

Printed in Europe, USA, Canada, Australia, Japan

Cover: Foto ©ninafisch / pixelio.de

More available books at **www.hansebooks.com**

TO THE

CITY OF CAMBRIDGE

MASSACHUSETTS

CONTENTS.

Part I.

CAMBRIDGE PUBLIC LIBRARY.

	PAGE
GIFT OF THE LIBRARY BUILDING	7
PROGRAMME OF THE EXERCISES AT THE DEDICATION	11
PROCEEDINGS	13
Presentation of the Deed by Colonel F. J. Parker	13
Mayor Gilmore's Response in accepting the Deed	18
Hon. S L Montague's Response	22
President Eliot's Address	23
Remarks by S. S. Green, Esq.	24
T. W. Higginson's Address	26
DESCRIPTION OF THE LIBRARY BUILDING	28

Part II.

THE MANUAL TRAINING SCHOOL.

GIFTS OF THE MANUAL TRAINING SCHOOL BUILDING AND THE CITY HALL	31
DESCRIPTION OF THE MANUAL TRAINING SCHOOL BUILDING	34

CONTENTS.

Part III.

THE CITY HALL.

	PAGE
LAYING THE CORNER-STONE	39
Mayor Gilmore's Address	41
Contents of Box	44
Address of M. W. G. M. Henry Endicott	46
Speech of Hon. W. E. Russell	48
Remarks by T. W. Higginson	52
Remarks by General Edward W. Hincks	54
TRANSFER OF THE CITY HALL TO THE CITY	57
Remarks by Colonel Parker	58
Remarks by Colonel Higginson	59
Mayor Gilmore's Speech	61
Transfer to the Committee on Public Property	65
Chairman Frasier's Response	66
DESCRIPTION OF THE CITY HALL BUILDING	67
NOTE	77

LIST OF ILLUSTRATIONS.

THE PUBLIC LIBRARY	*To face page* 7
THE TABLETS	" " 29
THE MANUAL TRAINING SCHOOL . . .	" " 31
THE ENTRANCE TO THE MANUAL TRAINING SCHOOL	" " 34
THE CITY HALL	" " 39
THE MAIN ENTRANCE TO THE CITY HALL .	" " 67

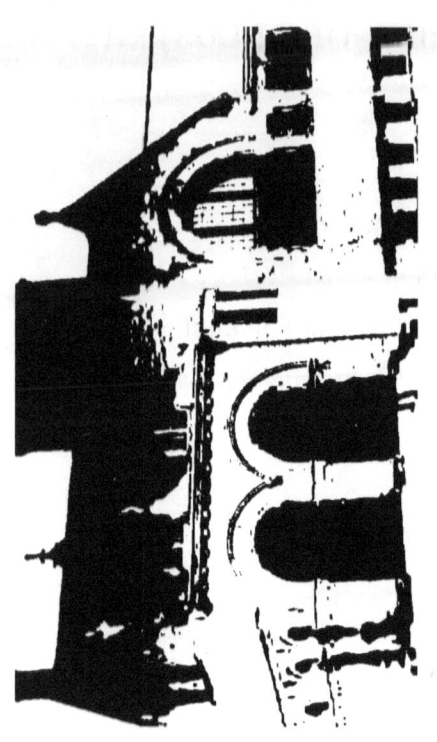

BUILT IN GRATITUDE TO GOD, TO HIS SON JESUS CHRIST, AND TO THE HOLY GHOST.

Commandments.

1
Thou shalt have no other gods before me.

2
Thou shalt not make unto thee any graven image, or any likeness of any thing that is in heaven above, or that is in the earth beneath, or that is in the water under the earth; thou shalt not bow down thyself to them, nor serve them: for I the Lord thy God am a jealous God, visiting the iniquity of the fathers upon the children unto the third and fourth generation of them that hate me; and shewing mercy unto thousands of them that love me, and keep my commandments.

3
Thou shalt not take the name of the Lord thy God in vain; for the Lord will not hold him guiltless that taketh his name in vain.

4
Remember the sabbath day to keep it holy. Six days shalt thou labour, and do all thy work: but the seventh day is the sabbath of the Lord thy God: in it thou shalt not do any work, thou, nor thy son, nor thy daughter, thy manservant, nor thy maidservant, nor thy cattle, nor thy stranger that is within thy gates. For in six days the Lord made heaven and earth, the sea, and all that in them is, and rested the seventh day: wherefore the Lord blessed the sabbath day, and hallowed it.

5
Honour thy father and thy mother: that thy days may be long upon the land which the Lord thy God giveth thee.

6
Thou shalt do no murder.

7
Thou shalt not commit adultery.

8
Thou shalt not steal.

9
Thou shalt not bear false witness against thy neighbour.

10
Thou shalt not covet thy neighbour's house, thou shalt not covet thy neighbour's wife, nor his manservant, nor his maidservant, nor his ox, nor his ass, nor any thing that is thy neighbour's.

11
Thou shalt love thy neighbour as thyself.

MEN, WOMEN, CHILDREN: IF YOU OBEY THESE COMMANDS YOU WILL BE HAPPY. IF YOU DISOBEY THEM, SORROW AWAITS YOU.

IT IS NOBLE TO BE PURE.
IT IS RIGHT TO BE HONEST.
IT IS NECESSARY TO BE TEMPERATE.
IT IS WISE TO BE INDUSTRIOUS:
BUT TO KNOW GOD IS BEST OF ALL.

PAUL THE APOSTLE BESOUGHT MEN TO PRESENT THEIR BODIES A LIVING SACRIFICE HOLY AND ACCEPTABLE UNTO GOD. THE BODY MUST NOT BE DISHONORED BY IMPURE ACTS. WISE ARE THEY WHO PROTECT THE PURITY OF THEIR BLOOD AND PRESERVE THEIR STRENGTH BY LIVING PURE LIVES.

THE TABLETS.

THE RINDGE GIFTS.

Part I.

CAMBRIDGE PUBLIC LIBRARY.

AT a regular meeting of the Board of Aldermen, held on June 15, 1887, it was stated by His Honor MAYOR RUSSELL that a communication of importance had been addressed to him by FREDERICK H. RINDGE, Esq., formerly of Cambridge, but now of Los Angeles, California; and at his suggestion a proposition was sent to the Common Council, for a joint convention to consider the subject of this communication. The joint convention was then held in the council-chamber. The Mayor presided, and spoke substantially as follows:—

I have called the members in joint convention for the purpose of announcing a gift, the most generous, the most useful, and the most public-spirited that the old city has yet received in the course of its history. Some of the members know that there is a Public Library, and some know that its present quarters are not adequate and hinder its usefulness; it has never had a proper place to live in.

The want of a Public Library building is felt every year, — it has been felt for many years. The subject has occupied the thought of a number of citizens who have sought to find a remedy. At a meeting of gentlemen interested, a short time ago, a committee of ten was appointed to talk over the matter to wealthy, generous, and public-spirited citizens, for the purpose of finding means to build a Public Library. I am most happy to say that not long since, as executive of this city, I made known the want of the city to one who, although he has not been a citizen of the city all his life, has always manifested a deep interest in its welfare. His generosity and Christian faith can more readily be told in his letter, which I will read to you.

BOSTON, June 14, 1887.

HON. WILLIAM E. RUSSELL.

DEAR SIR, — It would make me happy to give the city of Cambridge the tract of land bounded by Cambridge, Trowbridge, Broadway, and Irving Streets, in the city of Cambridge, and to build thereon and give to said city a Public Library building, under the following conditions : —

That on or within said building, tablets be placed bearing the following words : —

First — " Built in gratitude to God, to his son Jesus Christ, and to the Holy Spirit."

Second — The Ten Commandments and " Thou shalt love thy neighbor as thyself."

Third — " Men, women, children, obey these laws. If you do, you will be happy ; if you disobey them, sorrow will come upon you."

Fourth — " It is noble to be pure ; it is right to be honest ; it is necessary to be temperate ; it is wise to be industrious : but to know God is best of all."

Fifth — Words for this tablet to be given hereafter.

It is my wish that a portion of said tract of land be reserved as a playground for children and the young. I ask you to present this communication to the City Government of Cambridge and notify me of its action in relation to it. Should the gift be accepted, I hope to proceed at once with the work.

Yours respectfully,

FREDERICK H. RINDGE.

The Mayor then said that he had received another letter from Mr. Rindge, which read as follows: —

BOSTON, June 15, 1887.

HON. WILLIAM E. RUSSELL.

DEAR SIR, — Should the city of Cambridge accept my gift of land and Public Library building, I suggest that a committee composed of the following named citizens of Cambridge be appointed by the City Government of Cambridge to confer with my agent, Mr. Francis J. Parker, in matters relating to the accomplishment of the purposes of the building and land, — Mr. Justin Winsor, Col. T. W. Higginson, Hon. Samuel L. Montague, Hon. William E. Russell.

Yours respectfully,

FREDERICK H. RINDGE.

The Mayor continued, —

The tract of land contains nearly 115,000 square feet. It is bounded 224 feet each on Broadway and Cambridge Streets, 590 feet on Trowbridge Street, and 520 feet on Irving Street. He desires, and I think it would at once meet the approbation of the city, that the land should be laid out as a public park; it is amply large for that purpose. In regard to the building, I will say it will cost between $70,000 and $80,000, and will be as artistically built and as beautiful as could be erected on the lot. The plans have been prepared, and are at present in the hands of Mr. Rindge's agent. Mr. Rindge goes to California Friday; he leaves his property and affairs in charge of Mr. Parker. I suggest that immediate action be taken in the matter. I have prepared a set of resolutions, which I beg to present to the Board. They are as follows : —

Resolved, That the city of Cambridge accepts with profound gratitude the munificent gift of Mr. Frederick H. Rindge, of land and buildings for a public library as stated in his letter of June 14, 1887; that the city accepts it upon the conditions stated in said letter, which it will faithfully and gladly observe as a sacred trust, in accordance with his desire.

Resolved, That in gratefully accepting this gift, the city tenders to Frederick H. Rindge its heartfelt thanks and desires to express its sense of deep obligation to him, recognizing the Christian faith, generosity, and public spirit that have prompted him to supply a long-felt want by this gift of great and permanent usefulness.

The convention then dissolved. Upon the reassembling of each of the Boards, the resolutions were unanimously adopted, and by a unanimous vote in both Boards the gentlemen whose names are mentioned in the letter were invited to serve on the Committee.

The citizens designated to act on the Committee met and organized, and subsequently held many meetings. Proposals were ultimately issued for competing plans for a Library building, and after ample deliberation, — the plans being all sent to Mr. Rindge in California, — Messrs. Van Brunt and Howe were selected as architects. Ground was broken for the new Public Library on May 1st, 1888, and the building, when nearly completed, was dedicated, with public services, on June 29, 1889, on which day the keys of the new building were transferred to the city government. The following was the programme of the exercises : —

EXERCISES

AT THE

DEDICATION OF THE CAMBRIDGE PUBLIC LIBRARY.

SATURDAY, JUNE 29, 1889, AT 3 O'CLOCK, P. M.

PROGRAMME.

FESTIVAL TE DEUM, IN E FLAT . . . . *Dudley Buck.*
Quartet.

INVOCATION.
BY REV. ALEXANDER MCKENZIE, D. D.

PRESENTATION OF THE DEED OF GIFT FROM FREDERICK H. RINDGE,
TOGETHER WITH THE KEYS OF THE BUILDING.
BY COL. FRANCIS J. PARKER.

ACCEPTANCE OF THE GIFT
And transfer of the Keys of the Building to the Trustees of the Cambridge Public Library.
BY THE MAYOR, HON. HENRY H. GILMORE.

RESPONSE.

BY HON. SAMUEL L. MONTAGUE,
President of the Board of Trustees.

Anthem: HARK, HARK, MY SOUL! . . . . *Shelley.*
Quartet.

REMARKS.

BY CHARLES W. ELIOT,
President of Harvard University.

REMARKS.

BY SAMUEL S. GREEN,
Librarian of the Worcester Public Library.

Anthem: CANTATE DOMINO, IN C . . . . *Dudley Buck.*
"O, sing unto the Lord a new song,
For He hath done marvellous things."
Quartet.

REMARKS.

BY THOMAS WENTWORTH HIGGINSON.

The exercises will conclude by singing the DOXOLOGY, in which the audience is requested to join.

QUARTET.

MISS EDITH ESTELLE TORREY, *Soprano.*   GEORGE W. BARNES, *Tenor.*
MISS MINNIE G. HILLMAN, *Contralto.*   FRANCIS L PRATT, *Basso.*
MISS EMMA L. TAYLOR, *Pianist.*

PROCEEDINGS.

THE proceedings at the dedication of the CAMBRIDGE PUBLIC LIBRARY took place in the main hall-way in front of the delivery desk, a raised platform having been constructed for the rostrum. Mayor GILMORE and the invited speakers occupied the first row of chairs behind the desk, in the rear of them being the other special guests, such as the clergy and members of the City Government. A bouquet of flowers set off the speaker's desk, and, with an American flag across the window over the platform, formed the simple yet symbolic decorations of the day.

The exercises opened with the singing of Dudley Buck's Te Deum in E flat by the quartet. The accompanist was Miss Emma L. Taylor. Rev. Dr. McKENZIE then offered prayer, which was followed by the presentation of the deed and keys of the building from Frederick H. Rindge to the city, through Mayor Gilmore, by Col. FRANCIS J. PARKER.

PRESENTATION OF THE DEED BY COLONEL F. J. PARKER.

It has been fortunate for me, Your Honor, that my business relations with Mr. Rindge have devolved upon me many agreeable duties, and not the least pleasant of them is that which brings me here to-day. The Committee which has had the responsible charge of the construction and equipment of this beautiful building will tell you that everything that they have advised for the purpose of making it more complete has met the ready assent of the generous builder; and that he has even outrun their expressed wishes by authorizing expenditures which they did not suggest, until all, as you now see it, is complete, to the door-mat at the entrance and the shrubs upon the lawn. What your Committee will not tell you, is that you have before you now the result of a problem which for its solution required patient study, based upon special knowledge, good taste, sound judgment, wise foresight, and time-consuming pains; and that all these have been placed at your service by these gentlemen without recompense or profit to themselves. Cambridge owes much to this Committee. Since you called upon me a few days since, Mr. Mayor, to represent Mr. Rindge on this occasion, I have conversed with him across the continent, and have obtained his permission to read to you here a paper prepared for a different purpose, but which, as expressing his own ideas connected with his gifts to your city, you will, I am sure, be pleased to have me read: —

"All blessings come from God. Under Him, the people of Cambridge will owe the Manual Training School, the Public Library building, and the new City Hall to certain virtues which my parents possessed in an honorable degree, — the virtues temperance and industry, — and also to the desire of the donor to obey the new commandment given by our Lord Jesus Christ.

"I am persuaded that had my father lived until now, he would have made some such gifts to Cambridge, and that I have used a portion of the wealth which he amassed in a way that would have met his cordial approval; so that it is in his stead that I have devoted so much, and in such manner, to the use and benefit of his fellow-citizens.

THE RINDGE GIFTS.

"I regret that my father did not in his lifetime give more money for God's glory and for philanthropic purposes; and in saying this it must not be supposed that I am lacking in filial love and duty, for to my mind there are few men possessed of hearts kinder than my father's. But if he who by years of toil, through seasons of deep anxiety, accumulated a fortune, had himself expended a moiety of it in good works, the satisfaction would have been a high reward to him, and the act would have been one of great generosity.

"It is easier for one who has inherited wealth to disburse it for public purposes than for one who has earned it by sweat of body or brain; for the latter values it at what it has cost, — that is, perhaps, at a lifetime of continuous exertion; and the mental habits incident to million-making are very engrossing, and therefore tend to the constant postponement of acts of duty and of liberal intention. My father's last illness was sudden and short; it prevented even testamental provisions such as I believe he would otherwise have made.

"From what he gathered together, and what by rule of law has come from him to me, I, who had no share in the pains and labor of accumulation, may ungrudgingly, and as a duty, bestow a portion as he would have liked that I should do.

"But these gifts are also the return to God of what belongs to him and his purposes.

"It may be asked why so much has been given to one city; why I have not distributed my gifts more widely. Cambridge was my father's and mother's home, and my own birthplace. The recollections of my boyhood centre about it. On what is now the Public Library common I used to play ball and climb the hawthorn for its berries, which taste good to boys. Then, too, I believe that what is worth doing at all is worth doing well and thoroughly, and that concentration increases the power for good of gifts made or work done in the fear of God. Beyond all this, Cambridge has an important influence upon our whole country, and impressions made upon the minds of youth of other States temporarily living within her borders will in many cases be lasting, and thus bring good to other sections of our land.

"Some have marvelled at my desire to have inscriptions

placed in or upon each of the buildings, and some have wondered at the nature of the inscriptions.

"The attempt to make public buildings didactic is no novelty, as witness those of ancient Greece, Rome, and Egypt. Many of the churches near Cambridge are inscribed, inwardly or outwardly, with pious texts and solemn phrases. Many of the buildings owned by Harvard College bear its two mottoes, so that even on its secular buildings you may see the dedication to 'Truth' and 'To Christ and the Church.' Public buildings of Boston abound with the city motto, which is a prayer in Latin that 'God may be unto us as unto our fathers;' and according to an old custom, now happily reviving, it is not uncommon for him who builds a home to bless it or cheer it with scripture words.

"I have tried to place upon these new buildings in Cambridge sentences apt to their positions and such as all Christians could approve. Each is intended to assert a truth; and thus each building becomes in a sense a monument to truth, — the *veritas* of Harvard's escutcheon.

"It is hoped that these didactic buildings may in some degree impress upon those who see them these several truths: —

"*First*, that the commandments of our God are the only safe basis for education or government, and that obedience to them is needful for happiness.

"*Second*, that the office of administering government is an honorable service.

"*Third*, that a well-governed state or municipality implies the enforcement of its laws.

"*Fourth*, that honest occupation is a merit, and work a blessing.

"*Fifth*, that our youth should be instructed, not merely in things that train the mind, but also in those that will preserve and strengthen their souls and bodies.

"*Sixth*, that purity of mind and body is required alike by the laws of Nature and the command of Nature's God.

"To teach these truths is to help in perpetuating those private and civic virtues for which our New England forefathers were justly celebrated; to aid in the restoration of those types of manly health and womanly grace which are disappearing

THE RINDGE GIFTS. 17

from among our people; to oppose the growing idea that idleness is a mark of social advance, and money-getting the chief end of man. In short, to enforce upon the attention of men and women, young men and maidens, schoolboys and city councillors, those lessons of religion, patriotism, industry, and education by which if our lives are ruled, we may attain faith, peace, health, and prosperity.

"I know that if, in early youth, I had been impressed with the importance of these lessons, I should have avoided many wrong paths, and should have been spared many sorrows. As it was, I wavered and stumbled among the fallacies of certain philosophies, and unwittingly passed by the source from which men like Milton and Dante derived their highest inspiration, — those Holy Scriptures which have been alike the treasury of the wise and the comfort of the simple in all generations of the Christian era.

"Having fixed faith in the usefulness of didactic public buildings, I gratefully give these to my native city, that they may begin and follow their mission to promote faith, happiness, and peace. The truths on their tablets touch the interests of every one, and will, I trust, appeal to many a heart, help to strengthen many a wavering mind, and stir up noble thoughts and purposes in many a soul.

"It is my earnest request that no statue or memorial tablets be ever placed in the library building or on the lands which surround it.

"I have sought to make them monuments of the Truth and nothing else, and I would not that this purpose should be dimmed, or this power of teaching be diminished.

"I rejoice in these structures, not as one who has given anything, but as one who has received the bounty of God. My only regret is that they were not built by one worthier than myself."

This may be considered as Mr. Rindge's presentation message to his old fellow-townsmen and neighbors; and it only remains for me, as his agent, to deliver to you, as the chief magistrate, the deed which transfers to your city this Public Library building, its furniture and equipment, and the broad plaza on which it stands. May God prosper the giver and the gift, and its new owner, the good city of Cambridge, over which, Mr. Mayor, you so worthily preside! The deed of gift is in the ordinary legal form. After reciting the boundaries of the land, — " northerly by Cambridge Street, easterly by Trowbridge Street, southerly by Broadway, and westerly by Irving Street," — Mr. Rindge says, —

"On the wall of one of the public rooms of that building I have caused to be placed tablets of stone, on which are engraved the Ten Commandments and other sentences; and the city of Cambridge, by its acceptance of this deed, agrees that those tablets shall be maintained forever in the same position, or in case of any alteration or reconstruction of the building, then in some equally public and conspicuous position in the Library building, as altered or reconstructed. If it is consistent with other uses, I shall be glad to have some portion of the land reserved as a playground for young children; and if the city of Cambridge shall desire at any time to erect upon the premises additional buildings, to be occupied as a museum of art, or halls for lectures, or some kindred purpose, I assent to such use; but I do not intend that any portion of the land hereby conveyed shall be used for any of the purposes of ordinary city business, such as a site for a city hall, or a police-station, or even for a school-house. I do not choose to embarrass this conveyance by making it a condition of this deed that these expressions of my wishes should be observed, preferring to leave it entirely to the honor of the people and officers of my native town to see that those wishes, as above stated, are respected."

Mayor GILMORE, in accepting the gift, said: —

LADIES, GUESTS, AND FELLOW-CITIZENS, — The performance of no more agreeable duty can fall to the lot of any public official than is required of me at this time in accepting, as I do, in the name and on behalf of our good city of Cambridge, the title-deed to this beautiful park, enclosed by

THE RINDGE GIFTS.

four thoroughfares, and this building, so elegant, attractive, and convenient within, so stately and ornamental without; this ideal Public Library building; this perfect gem, — a noble and princely gift.

The occasion is made more felicitous, sir, by reason of your presence, the trusted friend and adviser, through whom Mr. Rindge formally transfers the fee in this valuable estate. It will add to the general satisfaction if you will graciously convey to him, whose absence from these ceremonies alone causes regret, and whose munificence has led up to this day of exuberant joy, an expression of something of the pleasure, of the pride, of the deep sense of gratitude felt by all of our citizens in the possession of this great benefaction.

These sentiments will be more adequately and eloquently expressed by others, who have in a fraternal spirit of goodwill and good fellowship honored this service with their presence.

The wish that has for years been so frequently expressed; the hope which has been so persistently entertained; the faith that has never wavered, though long suffering, — that Cambridge might have a Public Library building worthy of her name and of her people, has here and now met with grand fruition.

Summoned and assembled in this place are all the æsthetic conditions and surroundings calculated to attract young and old, of every condition in life. The artistic eye will find here gratifications in viewing proportions carefully studied; coloring and finish challenging the most critical taste.

The practical observer will detect solidity, — the bending of means to the best ends, the conservation of space, and the general adaptability of the whole plan for uses subject to its design. The visitor of tender years, or others of uneducated perceptions, cannot fail to have aroused within them the desire to attain sufficient knowledge, through the aids available from this source to make their conceptions more nearly approach their opportunities.

This is undoubtedly the aim and purpose of Mr. Rindge. With that generous confidence in the honor and fidelity of his fellow-men which distinguishes him above any other man, he places no restrictions upon the trustees of the Cambridge Public Library, under whose sole care and control he desires this building to be placed, notwithstanding they are to him personally unknown. He implicitly relies upon them to manage its affairs faithfully, to fill its shelves with literature worthy of the age, to offer its sheltering arms to every traveller in pursuit of intellectual improvement.

I have no warrant for it, but I do believe it would consort with his wishes if all proper means were applied to win the young to its fold, especially those who have few advantages, and are the most distant from sources of mental culture, and whose future usefulness to the state so largely depends upon elevating them to a condition where the desire to gain education will result in their becoming happy, useful, and respected citizens.

That the student, the persons more deeply read, will avail of the opportunities to refresh their minds and to gather the rich fruitage, cultivated and ripened by active minds in all ages, we do not doubt.

Let all enter, assured of a welcome, of attention, and of assistance if needed or required. Let the manifestation of an honest desire to take advantage of the privileges of this library, an evident disposition to labor and to merit approval, always have courteous recognition and be regarded as the open sesame to its most precious treasures. There are possessions richer than gold. He only is possessed of true wealth whose mind is well stored and disciplined, with

THE RINDGE GIFTS.

whom refinement is a virtue, honor a prerequisite, and whose aspirations reach humbly, actively, and trustingly towards the source of infinite knowledge.

Fellow-citizens, whilst we rejoice in adding this gem to the necklace of our beloved city, let us also renew our pledges of loyalty to her, and resolve, by well directed and constant efforts, to raise her to such a moral and intellectual elevation that envy shall be disarmed and detraction shall not reach her.

Turning to Hon. S. L. Montague, President of the Board of Trustees, the Mayor continued: —

MR. PRESIDENT OF THE BOARD OF TRUSTEES OF THE CAMBRIDGE PUBLIC LIBRARY, — I am in possession of a letter written to me by Mr. Rindge, which accompanied the deed of gift, that deserves to be known to every resident of Cambridge; and I read it to you now, that his request "that the care and control of the Public Library building be ever under the direction of the Trustees of said Library," may be brought to your attention: —

LOS ANGELES, June 14, 1889.

HON. HENRY H. GILMORE.

DEAR SIR, — I send herewith a deed conveying to the city of Cambridge the Public Library common and the Public Library building. I have added to the deed a request that the care and control of the Public Library building be ever under the direction of the Trustees of said Library. Will you kindly present this request to the City Government of Cambridge for their consideration, and notify me of its action in relation to it.

I anticipate with much pleasure the time when I shall see the new Cambridge buildings completed and in active usefulness. There remains nothing to be written, I believe, except that the deepest good-will of my heart goes with the deed.

Yours respectfully,

FREDERICK H. RINDGE.

In deference to his wish, the Honorable City Council, on June 25, passed this order, with entire unanimity : —

Ordered, that the Public Library building be placed in charge of the Trustees of the Cambridge Public Library, which Board shall have full control over the care and repairs of the same.

It is therefore my happy privilege to put into your hands the keys, and to place this building, through you, in the care and custody of the Board of Trustees, that it may by them be made to exert the " active usefulness " designed by our friend and patron, Frederick H. Rindge.

HON. S. L. MONTAGUE'S RESPONSE.

Hon. SAMUEL L. MONTAGUE, in responding for the Board of Trustees, said : —

If I were able, it would not be wise for me to attempt to make any extended remarks at this time. The eminent gentlemen who are to follow me are so much better fitted to speak on the great question of how to make a free public library of the greatest benefit to the community that anything that I could say would sound weak and out of place by comparison ; and I shall leave to my associate, Colonel Higginson, to speak for the Trustees of their plans and purposes in regard to the future management of the Library.

And now, Mr. Mayor, I will simply perform my official duty, as Chairman of the Board of Trustees of the Cambridge Public Library, and formally accept on their behalf the keys and custody of this beautiful building, and will pledge, for each and every one of us, that as far as we are able we will administer its affairs so that it shall ever serve the noble purpose which Mr. Rindge had in view when he made this munificent gift to our city.

THE RINDGE GIFTS.

The quartet followed with an anthem, "Hark, hark, my Soul!" by Shelley; after which the Mayor introduced CHARLES W. ELIOT, President of Harvard University, who spoke as follows: —

PRESIDENT ELIOT'S ADDRESS.

MR. MAYOR, LADIES AND GENTLEMEN, — I can wish for Mr. Rindge no better immediate reward than the full vision of what a free library may do for a community. Public libraries, circulating libraries, Sunday-school libraries, and book-clubs, nowadays, bring much reading to the door of every household and of every solitary creature that wants to read. This is a new privilege for the mass of mankind, and it is an inexhaustible source of intellectual and spiritual nutriment. We hardly begin to realize what a free library's influence may be on the coming generations.

Once when I was talking with Dr. Oliver Wendell Holmes about the best pleasures in life, he mentioned, as one of the most precious, frequent contact with well-stored minds in large variety. He valued highly the number, frequency, and variety of quickening intellectual encounters. We were thinking of contact in conversation; but this pleasure, if only to be procured by personal meetings, would obviously be within the reach, as a rule, of only a very limited number of persons. We cannot all see and talk with Holmes, Lowell, and Whittier face to face. I suppose it will be much the same in the kingdom of heaven. We may not all be able to hold converse there with Plato, Michael Angelo, Luther, and Shakspeare. Fortunately for us and for posterity, the printing-press and the library bring within easy reach of every man who can read all the best minds both of the past and the present.

Books are the quietest and the most constant of friends;

they are the most accessible and wisest of counsellors, and the most patient of teachers. With his daily work and his books, many a man whom the world thought forlorn has found life worth living.

It is a mistake to suppose that a great deal of leisure is necessary for this happy intercourse with books. Ten minutes a day devoted affectionately to good books — indeed, to one book of the first order, like the English Bible or Shakspeare, or to two or three books of the second order, like Homer, Virgil, Milton, or Bacon — will, in thirty years, make all the difference between a cultivated and an uncultivated man; between a man mentally rich and a man mentally poor. The pleasures of reading are, of course, in good part, pleasures of the imagination; but they are just as actual and natural as pleasures of the senses, and are often more accessible and more lasting. Let no one hesitate to use this Library, if only for fifteen minutes at a time. Hold communion, if only for fifteen minutes a week, with the great intellects of the world.

Free public libraries are scarcely more than one generation old; yet they are already among the chief of the potent forces which promote intelligence and righteousness in free communities. Let us wish for Mr. Rindge a full vision of the enduring and multiplying benefits which will certainly flow from his gift.

The next speaker was Mr. S. S. GREEN, the librarian of the Worcester Public Library, of whose remarks the following is an abstract: —

REMARKS BY S. S. GREEN, ESQ.

Many persons seem to think that public libraries are merely storehouses of novels. This is not the case, however. Still, novels and stories play an important part in the cultivation of the imagination, in awakening the feelings, in exerting a healthful moral influence, and in affording rational enjoyment.

The main purpose of the establishment of public libraries is to afford facilities for instruction. Encouragement should be given for the acquisition of knowledge for its own sake; but, said Mr. Green, "when I stand before an audience made up, as the one here is, mainly of men and women who are engaged in active pursuits, I like to show that a public library is of great value to persons whose lives are spent in doing every-day duties."

Mr. Green proceeded to give several instances, selected from many that had come under his observation, of advantages which had come to farmers and mechanics who used freely books and papers treating of subjects connected with their occupations.

He also showed that very valuable results follow a considerable use of library books by teachers and scholars in schools, pointing out how they could be used to advantage in connection with studies, and stating that he knew of teachers who, without the exercise of force, and only by exciting interest in subjects, controlled almost entirely the home reading of large numbers of their scholars. He expressed the opinion that thousands of library books might be used to advantage daily in connection with school work either in school, or at home in this city.

Mr. Green spoke of the habit of reading and of the public library as allies of the promotion of good morals; and in alluding to the mottoes on the wall, said that just as the influence of the teacher was of more value in making good boys and girls than the public reading of the Bible in the school, so the real power of the library for exerting a beneficial moral influence depended upon the atmosphere which pervaded the institution and the spirit which guided the librarian and directors in the selection of books and the administration of the affairs of the library.

In conclusion, Mr. Green expressed his indebtedness and gratitude to his alma mater, Harvard College.

The quartet then sang the anthem, "Cantate Domino," in C, by Dudley Buck.

T. W. HIGGINSON'S ADDRESS.

The speaker began by saying that the event which brought the audience before him together was a happy one for all citizens, and the fulfilment of a dream which seemed almost too good to be true. Nevertheless, the Library stood in its place complete. The people would find it there to-morrow, and their children's children would also find it there. The dream was, after all, a reality. He regretted the absence of Ex-Mayor Russell, and said that the people should never think of the Library as due to the beneficence of Mr. Rindge alone, but also to the fact that his classmate, our young ex-mayor, by one of the rare strokes of good fortune which, as Emerson says, happen only to good players, was able to bring to his attention, at just the right time, the needs of the city.

"To the Cambridge Club, also, from which came the first suggestion of the new building," said the speaker, "to the architect, to Mr. Justin Winsor, and to the librarian, who repeatedly has urged upon our people the necessities of the case, our thanks are due. The fact is, we have so much gratitude that we want to spread it out over as many people as we can.

"We are now the possessors of this beautiful structure. Yesterday it was Mr. Rindge's; to-day it is ours. We are to use it as our own. It belongs to the people. There are rules and restrictions, — as there must be, — but only to make it more thoroughly and truly ours. Think how much more far-reaching the library is than the schools! The latter take but a portion of the population, and for a few years of their lives. No such limitation surrounds the library. The poorest boy and the wisest university prosessor here shall sit down side by side."

The speaker then referred to the plans for distributing books from the Library to designated points in the city, and spoke, in closing, of the "Cambridge Memorial Rooms," designed to preserve memorials of the literature, art, and history of this community.

The exercises were brought to a close with the singing of the Doxology and a benediction by Rev. ALEXANDER MCKENZIE, D. D.

DESCRIPTION

OF

THE LIBRARY BUILDING.

THE building is composed of two main divisions, — the one, partially fire proof, being devoted to the convenience of the public and to the administration of the Library; the other to the absolute fire-proof storage of the books. The former includes a large public waiting hall, a reading hall with reference library, and memorial and administration rooms. The entrance porch is in the southwest corner of the building, and gives access to the vestibule and entrance hall, which opens directly into the delivery hall, from which, on the axis of the entrance hall, an archway gives communication with the reading room, which is finished with an apsidal projection toward the east, and communicates with the cataloguing room, which occupies a lean-to on the north side. From the entrance hall also access is obtained to the memorial rooms and to the staircase which communicates with the basement, wherein is located the janitor's room, men's toilet rooms, heating apparatus, etc., and with the second story, which contains a large class and study room and toilet rooms.

THE RINDGE GIFTS.

The delivery hall is thirty-one by forty-six feet, the longitudinal axis running north and south. It has an open timbered roof, and is furnished with catalogue counters, delivery desk, settees, and other equipments essential to the public service of the Library. The north wall of the delivery room contains tablets in various marbles, bearing inscriptions, dictated by Mr. Rindge, as follows: —

First — " Built in gratitude to God, to his son Jesus Christ, and to the Holy Spirit."

Second — The Ten Commandments and "Thou shalt love thy neighbor as thyself."

Third — " Men, women, children, obey these laws. If you do, you will be happy; if you disobey them, sorrow will come upon you."

Fourth — " It is noble to be pure; it is right to be honest; it is necessary to be temperate; it is wise to be industrious; but to know God is best of all."

Fifth — " Paul the Apostle besought men to present their bodies a living sacrifice holy and acceptable unto God.

" The body must not be dishonored by impure acts. Wise are they who protect the purity of their blood and preserve their strength by living pure lives."

All the public rooms are wainscoted with panelling in ash.

The book room is extended from the delivery room northward, having the same width; namely, thirty-one by thirty-six feet in length. This apartment, which is provided for a future extension northward, is entirely fire proof, and is separated from the main building by a fire wall. The present construction contains six transverse book racks of iron, separated by aisles three feet wide. Each rack is divided into eight divisions of three feet each, and the wing containing these stacks is divided by openwork floor-plates of iron into four stories, each eight feet high. Windows occur opposite each transverse aisle, and the most careful and scientific provisions are made for the equal ventilation of the apartment. This system of book stacks is devised to facilitate accessibility, classification, abundant light, and perfect dryness, in the most compact possible form. An iron staircase gives access to the several stories, and the communication with the main building through the fire wall is by fire-proof doors. The capacity of the portion of the book stack already built is about eighty thousand volumes, and plans have been provided for a future extension, which will double this accommodation when required.

The exterior of the building is in Dedham stone, with dark sandstone trimmings. In architectural expression the structure follows the Romanesque style of southern France, which admits of great wealth of carving and refinement of detail. The building is distinguished by a round tower for ventilation.

THE MANUAL TRAINING SCHOOL

HELIOTYPE PRINTING CO., BOSTON

Part II.

THE MANUAL TRAINING SCHOOL.

ON Nov. 12, 1887, a special meeting of both branches of the City Council was called by Mayor RUSSELL, at which he read the following letters from Mr. Rindge: —

LOS ANGELES, Nov. 3, 1887.
HON. WM. E. RUSSELL:

DEAR SIR, — It would make me happy to give the city of Cambridge, provided no considerable misfortune happens to my property within two years from date, three gifts, which are described herein.

First, a worthy site for a High School Building in the immediate neighborhood of the Public Library common, provided the following inscription, in metal or stone letters, be placed on the outside of said building and over the main entrance door: "Knowledge is worth seeking; but the wise, while striving to cultivate their minds, strive also to acquire strength of soul and body: then knowledge avails." And provided also one other condition, which shall be given hereafter, be complied with. [This condition is that an adjoining lot be purchased and added to the High School lot.]

Second, a City Hall, provided the following inscription, in metal or stone letters, be placed on the outside of said building and over its main entrance door: "God has given commandments unto men. From these commandments men have framed laws by which to be governed. It is honorable and praiseworthy faithfully to serve the people by helping to administer these laws. If the laws are not enforced, the people are not well governed." And provided also the city of Cambridge give a worthy site for said City Hall.

Third, an Industrial School Building ready for use, together with a site for the same in the immediate neighborhood of the Public Library common, provided the following inscription, in metal or stone letters, be placed on the outside of said building and over its main entrance door: " Work is one of our greatest blessings; every one should have an honest occupation." I wish the plain arts of industry to be taught in this school. I wish the school to be especially for boys of average talents, who may in it learn how their arms and hands can earn food, clothing, and shelter for themselves; how, after a while, they can support a family and a home; and how the price of these blessings is faithful industry, no bad habits, and wise economy, — which price, by the way, is not dear. I wish also that in it they may become accustomed to being under authority, and be now and then instructed in the laws that govern health and nobility of character. I urge that admittance to said school be given only to strong boys, who will grow up to be able working-men. Strict obedience to such a rule would tend to make parents careful in the training of their young, as they would know that their boys would be deprived of the benefits of said school unless they were able-bodied. I think the Industrial School would thus graduate many young men, who would prove themselves useful citizens. I ask you to present this communication to the City Government of Cambridge and notify me of its action in relation to it. Should the gifts, with their conditions, be accepted, I hope to proceed at once with the work.

Respectfully yours,

FREDERICK H. RINDGE.

LOS ANGELES, Nov. 3, 1887.

HON. WILLIAM E. RUSSELL:

DEAR SIR, — Should the city of Cambridge decide to accept the gifts, with their conditions, mentioned in my other communication of this date to said city, I suggest that the following named citizens of Cambridge be requested to act as a committee,

THE RINDGE GIFTS. 33

representing the city of Cambridge, to confer with my agent, Mr. Francis J. Parker, on matters relating to the accomplishment of the purposes of said gifts: Thomas W. Higginson, Epes S. Dixwell, Samuel L. Montague, Wm. E. Russell.

Yours respectfully,

FRED'K H. RINDGE.

After hearing the letters read, the Boards dissolved, and took action separately on the same. The Aldermen adopted the following resolution, after an expression of appreciation from several members of the Board: —

Resolved, That the city of Cambridge accepts with deep gratitude the munificent gifts of Mr. F. H. Rindge, as expressed in his letter of Nov. 3, 1887, to the Mayor. In accepting said gifts, it desires to signify to him its profound and lasting appreciation of his great generosity and public spirit.

In the Common Council the foregoing resolution was unanimously adopted in concurrence.

Mr. Epes S. Dixwell having declined, by reason of age, to serve on this Committee, — while expressing the utmost interest in its objects, — Mr. Harry Ellis was elected to act in his place. He had the main charge of the erection and equipment of the school; and there was no competition of architects, the planning of the building being intrusted by the Committee to Messrs. Rotch and Tilden, in connection with Mr. Ellis. Ground was broken July 12, 1888, and the building was ready for use on the first day of October following. No special dedicatory services were held, the building not being as yet transferred to the city.

DESCRIPTION

OF THE

MANUAL TRAINING SCHOOL BUILDING.

THE building is of a Romanesque style of architecture, and stands nearly in the geographical centre of the city, upon a generous lot at the corner of Broadway and Irving Street.

This structure, while by no means so immense in its proportions as the nearly finished English High School building, situated but a few hundred feet away, and while slightly inferior in ornamentation to its neighbor, the Public Library, nevertheless impresses the mind of the observer with its evident adaptability to the purpose for which it was intended; that is, the combination of manual and intellectual education.

Upon closer examination it is seen to be of three distinct parts; namely, a main building, with wings of equal proportions. The central portion is of two stories, and has a hip-roof, from the middle part of which rises a massive panelled chimney eighty feet high, surrounded near the top with an iron balcony. The overhanging eaves are supported by massive timbers, giving both strength and character to the building.

Upon either side of the front door, over which is inscribed the motto, "Work is one of our greatest blessings; every one should have an honest occupation," are two semicircular extensions, with conical tiled roofs; these extensions are used for office purposes.

The front doors, reached by generous brown-stone steps, are of quartered oak and of large dimensions, above which is a shapely tiled arch. This building is of brick, with Long-Meadow sandstone trimmings. Each of the wings is lighted by large semicircular windows, and also by roof windows.

The external proportions of the building are — the main part, seventy by sixty-two feet, and the wings, which are each sixty feet square.

The front part of the main building, upon the lower floor, finished in quartered oak, contains the offices necessary for a school of this character; the rear part of the main building being set aside for the forge room, which measures thirty-four by seventy feet.

This room contains fifteen forges, anvils, and all the necessary appliances for this kind of work. The boiler, which generates steam for the engine and for heating the entire building, is also placed in this room.

The southerly wing is devoted to wood-working. The room is used for two departments, — the east side being fitted for general carpentry, and the west side for turning and pattern-making. The former has eight wood-worker's benches, well arranged as regards light and convenience. Running the entire length of the west side of the room, near the windows is a bench supplied with pattern-making tools, and in front of the bench, at a convenient distance from it, a row of twelve pattern-making lathes. This room is also provided with band-saws, circular saws, grindstones, emery wheels, etc. It is finished entirely into the roof, and perfect lighting and ventilation are secured.

The northerly wing is in the main like the one described above. This room contains all appliances necessary for machine work, and also gives space to the engine, which supplies power for the entire building, and the dynamo, which generates the current for all the lighting. The shafting of the entire building is supported upon well-designed hard-pine trusses, and one is surprised at the absence of jarring frequently found in buildings containing so much machinery.

The westerly side of this room is devoted to benches for iron-fitting, while the opposite side is given up to machine work, lathes, planers, drills, etc., and also has upon its entire length next to the windows a bench used for the setting up of the machines which have been constructed by the pupils. A door leads from the southerly side into an ample tool room fitted with a large number of shelves and cases used for the storage of numerous tools employed in the shop work; each of these wings is separated from the main building by fire-proof walls and doors.

The basement provides toilet-rooms, wash-rooms, and two hundred and seventy-five lockers for the accommodation of the pupils' clothing, a large dining-room with a seating capacity for the entire school, the necessary kitchens, and store-rooms.

The second story of the main building is reached

by wooden platform stairs built of quartered oak, and contains two recitation rooms and a large drawing-room amply lighted by both side-windows and skylights, being fitted with the necessary benches, blue-print frames, and washing and drying stands, for blue-prints.

The whole building is so constructed that it may be readily enlarged by the raising of the roof of both the wings and the main part; and it is confidently predicted that such an enlargement will soon be necessary, on account of the great popularity which the school already enjoys, — thus proving how firm a foothold manual training has already secured as an educational factor in the school system, and how much it is appreciated by the citizens of Cambridge.

THE CITY HALL

Part III.

THE CITY HALL.

THE Committee of citizens under whose charge the City Hall was erected was identical with that having charge of the Manual Training School, with the addition of Mayor Gilmore, who by request of Mr. Rindge was appointed on the Committee on March 26, 1889; the chief duty being, however, performed by the two ex-mayors, Messrs. Montague and Russell, and his Honor Mayor Gilmore. The Committee issued proposals for the building, and the architects selected were Messrs. Longfellow, Alden, and Harlow. A site suitable to the purpose having been purchased by the City Government, — namely, all the land between Bigelow and Inman Streets running back about two hundred and thirty-five feet from Main Street, — ground was broken on Feb. 1, 1889, and the corner-stone of the building was laid, with appropriate ceremonies, on May 15, 1889, in presence of a large concourse of people. The day was very fine, and all the circumstances were propitious.

The guests of Mayor Gilmore, including Mayor Hart of Boston and upwards of two hundred citizens, assembled at the City Hall, and at the hour appointed marched to the site and took seats upon a platform that had been erected. Here also were seated several hundred ladies who had been fortunate enough to secure tickets of admission.

Meanwhile the members of the several Masonic Lodges had assembled in the vicinity of Central Square, and shortly before three o'clock, headed by Carter's Band, marched to the scene of the exercises. The Grand Lodge of Masons was represented by Most Worshipful Henry Endicott, Grand Master; his deputy, Samuel Wells; the Senior Grand Warden, Judge Andrew C. Stone, of Lawrence; the acting Junior Grand Warden, Dana J. Flanders (who officiated in the unavoidable absence of Junior Warden Henry G. Wood); the Grand Chaplain, Rev. Charles A. Skinner; the Grand Treasurer, John Carr; the Grand Marshal, George H. Rhodes; the Recording Grand Secretary, Sereno D. Nickerson; the Corresponding Grand Secretary, Prof. Benjamin A. Gould; Past Grand Master William Parkman; Rev. Lucius R. Paige, D.D., Hon. Frederick D. Ely, Judge Sanger; Past Senior Grand Wardens W. T. Grammer, W. H. Chessman, C. M. Avery, W. T. R. Marvin, and J. M. Gleason; Past Junior Grand Wardens Wyzeman Marshall, I. H. Pope, L. W. Lovell, Henry G. Fay, N. S. Kimball, Thomas W. Davis, W. H. H. Soule, George W. Storer, and Charles Harris.

The exercises opened with singing by the Temple quartet. Mayor GILMORE then requested the Grand Lodge of Masons to lay the corner-stone of the Hall, saying, —

THE RINDGE GIFTS.

MAYOR GILMORE'S ADDRESS.

LADIES AND GENTLEMEN, — On the morning of November 12, 1887, at a special meeting of the Honorable City Council, the city of Cambridge accepted the tender of three magnificent gifts. One of her worthy sons, recognizing the fact that his native city was breaking away from a comparatively inert past into an active, enterprising, and expanding present, that pressing needs were upon her, beyond her ability to meet without stepping outside the limits of taxation fixed by law, came forward, and in a spirit of liberality as uncommon as it is munificent, tendered to the city, as one of several benefactions, a new City Hall. Its minutest details of construction have been skilfully conceived, considered, and proportioned by architects of the highest rank. The builders, also noted for the excellence and thoroughness of their work, have thus far progressed. The solid foundations are in position before you, and the name of Frederick H. Rindge will be held in grateful recollection longer than this quarried granite shall withstand the ravages of time. The hum of prosperous industry, the clatter of street intercourse, wonderfully increased and improved by methods demonstrating the startling revolutions peculiar to the age in which we live, the activity displayed in building, the increased volume of trade and traffic, the evident signs of growth and material prosperity greeting the eye on every side, the call for park systems, the opening and projection of new bridges, streets, and avenues, are only the developments of a period that also demands accessories to attaining a higher mental range, together with wisely administered mechanical instrumentalities by which the right hand may be taught its cunning, thus uniting to better purpose, for grander results, the intellectual with the practical.

Viewed in this light, how admirable is the generous

conception of our young friend and benefactor! The gift of a park upon which the city will erect an elegant school building; the gift of a beautiful and attractive free Public Library building, with ample grounds; the erection of the Manual Training School building, and fitting it with the best classes of tools and machinery, within which, for a term of years, at his individual expense, is to be developed, free to the pupils, the most promising scheme of industrial education, a scheme so attractive, so meritorious, that it has, in a certain way, challenged the attention of "Fair Harvard," — and great hope for future mutual benefit may be based upon this fact.

Thrice blessed and happy is he whose possessions permit him liberally to contribute to measures, wisely considered, to be wholly devoted to the uses of the people and in their highest interest! Cambridge past is rich in tradition and history. She has acquisitions in which she feels justifiable pride. Her development has been steady, her improvements never premature. Good men and true have given and are giving to her faithful if gratuitous service, and she has had honest and good government. It may justly be claimed that municipal affairs in our good city have at least been as prudently, carefully, and ably managed as in any other New England city, and no tax-payer need feel any apprehension that his contribution to the fund to meet general expenses will be either squandered or misapplied.

Of Cambridge anon we may indulge the most pleasant and glowing anticipations. Who shall dare to plant bounds to her future greatness? It were perhaps idle to fancy to what breadth and height, to what rank, what importance and power she may attain. The intelligently applied energies of her people will be aroused — nay, they now are aroused — to make and keep our fair city fairer, to provide all possible facilities, conveniences, and advantages calculated to justify the claim we make for her as being, all in

THE RINDGE GIFTS. 43

all, the most beautiful and attractive city of homes in this broad land.

The Honorable City Council wisely determined that the corner-stone of the imposing edifice hereupon to be erected should be laid with formal and appropriate ceremonies, and this is the day and hour set apart for the purpose.

Most Worshipful Henry Endicott, Grand Master of the Most Worshipful Grand Lodge of Massachusetts, has kindly consented, with the aid of the right worshipful grand officers with him associated, to lay the head of the corner in the manner peculiar to ancient form.

It gives me great satisfaction and pleasure, in behalf of the authorities and the people of Cambridge, to welcome here and on this occasion these worthy representatives of those who in olden times " came up to Jerusalem to help, aid, and assist in the re-building of the house of the Lord, without the hope of fee or reward." To add to the dignity and importance of this undertaking, several distinguished citizens have accepted invitations to be present and participate in the observances of the hour, and in behalf of the Honorable City Council I bid you all a cordial and hearty welcome.

Within the massive superstructure hereafter to be dedicated to honest government, may substantial justice and impartiality control the executive action, the legislative bodies be governed by convictions broad, progressive, and wisely conservative! May every one to be officially connected with the public service enter it inspired with a laudable ambition to perform his whole duty, that he may, at the expiration of his term of service, depart with honor.

MOST WORSHIPFUL GRAND MASTER, — Having gratified and honored the people of Cambridge by appearing here, accompanied by the distinguished gentlemen who compose your suite, for the purpose of laying the corner-stone of this building, it is my agreeable privilege to make the request that you will now assume the direction of affairs, that the good work may be accomplished.

Grand Master ENDICOTT responded, saying that from the earliest inception of masonry, it had been a custom for lodges to lay the corner-stone of buildings for the purpose of administering good and pure government; and therefore the grand lodge can lay the corner-stone of this edifice, thereby testifying its respect for justice and good government.

The Grand Master then called on Grand Chaplain Rev. C. A. SKINNER to read the Scripture and invoke the divine blessing. City Clerk PIKE then handed to the Grand Master the box — which is $10\frac{3}{4}$ inches long, 7 inches wide, and 7 inches deep — to be deposited beneath the corner-stone, with a written list of the contents, which were in turn given over to the Grand Treasurer, R. W. JOHN CARR, with the request to read it. It contained the following articles:

CONTENTS OF BOX.

1. A map of the City of Cambridge, showing the division into wards and voting precincts as it exists to-day.
2. Copies of letters of Frederick H. Rindge, and the records of the City Council in relation thereto.
3. Copies of each of the weekly papers published in this city under date of May 11, 1889; a copy of the Y. M. C. A. "Record" for May.
4. A Cambridge Directory for the year 1889.
5. A copy of the record of the proceedings commemorating the two hundred and fiftieth anniversary of the settlement of Cambridge.

6. A copy of the Annual Report of the City of Cambridge for the year 1888.

7. A Report of the Cambridge Water Board for the year 1888.

8. A Report of the Overseers of the Poor for the year 1888.

9. A copy of the Charter and Ordinances of the City.

10. A map and description of the proposed improvements in the Charles River basin.

11. A copy of the order of exercises for the laying of the corner-stone.

12. A copy of the organization of the Most Worshipful Grand Lodge of Ancient, Free, and Accepted Masons of Massachusetts for the year 1889.

13. A copy of each of the ballots used at the municipal election in December, 1888.

The box was then deposited in the receptacle prepared for it. The Grand Master took the trowel, the Deputy Grand Master the square, the Senior Grand Warden the level, and the Junior Grand Warden the plumb, and assumed their respective positions about the corner-stone. The Grand Master then invited His Honor Mayor Gilmore and ex-mayors Allen, Fox, and Montague to assist in spreading the cement. The libations of corn, wine, and oil were then applied by the Deputy Grand Master Samuel Wells, Senior Grand Warden Andrew C. Stone, and Junior Grand Warden Dana J. Flanders respectively. The Grand Chaplain then made an invocation, and Grand Master Endicott presented the working tools to Architect Longfellow.

The GRAND MASTER then delivered the following address: —

ADDRESS OF M. W. G. M. HENRY ENDICOTT.

The fact that masonry is founded on truths that are universal, and not on the special needs of any one country, of any one race, or of any one religion, is shown by the facility with which it adapts itself to conditions that at first thought seem almost opposed to each other. Substantially the same ceremony that consecrated the corner-stones of those cathedrals that are the glory of Europe and the priceless inheritance from the Middle Ages, the same ceremony that symbolized truth to the early Christians, the same ceremony that inspired by its mystic rites the awe of the Assyrians and Egyptians, lends itself to us to-day as a fitting expression of those feelings with which we would have this building begun.

The very antiquity of the custom endears it to us. It shows us that we are one with the people of all the centuries that have gone before, that the feelings in our hearts to-day are much the same in essence as those of generations past, and we learn the old yet ever new lesson that God hath made of one blood all the nations of the earth.

A custom that has endured for thirty-six hundred years must strike its roots deep into the universal soil of human nature, and is perpetuated by no useless regard for custom.

The ancient Egyptians believed that when man had done his share of the work, then the hand of God seized the hammer, and by giving the final blow laid the stone true. To-day, with widely different conceptions, do we none the less truly recognize the divine power that speaks through the growing thoughts and deeds of man. We know to-day that every building serves the divine purpose which answers to the needs of civilization and may help advance the welfare of humanity. That the building which is to stand in this place will do this, we firmly believe, and thus with earnestness and reverence have we laid its corner-stone.

A few days ago we celebrated the centennial of our government. We looked back through the years in the century past.

Memories of the early struggles of our fathers, memories of the war which devastated many homes and brought many anxious hours, mingled with thoughts of the future to which our country is destined. We can see clearly from this vantage-ground of one hundred years how, even in spite of danger and discouragement, a high ideal has stood before the people, leading them on. Our problems are far from being settled. We cannot yet fold our hands and believe that right will prosper without the help of honest-hearted men. We need less zeal for party and more for our country, we need less luxury and more intelligence, less form and more substance ; and yet, in spite of every discouraging fact, we can see that this ideal has never vanished. Perhaps we might say that it has never even lost ground.

We dream of that republic " where, from sea to sea, the people shall be wise and good and free," and we take fresh courage to work towards the realization of that ideal. Now this building is to help us in that direction.

Cambridge stands in the foremost line of progress. Its honored names are heard wherever the English language is spoken, and not in one language alone are resung the songs of its poets. Harvard University sends its sons into every part of the world and influences life in places whose very names are unknown to us to-day.

We have been endowed with noble gifts by the munificence of a single citizen. Let this building, which is to be raised through his generosity, be devoted to the highest uses. As the corner-stone has been laid square, let justice approve the administration of affairs in this place; as it has been laid level, let the thought of the brotherhood of man be ever present here, and let every citizen of Cambridge appreciate his own share of responsibility for the right government of our city; as it has been laid plumb, let absolute honesty and uprightness be the aim of all whose footsteps turn this way, and distinguish all public measures. May this building stand through years of peace and plenty, not only adding new dignity to our fair city, but as the fitting emblem of a free government of a free people.

At the conclusion of the Grand Master's address, speeches were made by Ex-Mayor WILLIAM E. RUSSELL, THOMAS WENTWORTH HIGGINSON, and General EDWARD W. HINCKS.

SPEECH OF HON. W. E. RUSSELL.

MR. MAYOR, LADIES AND GENTLEMEN, — With much pleasure I have come to these exercises to express in a few words my interest in the progress of this work, in whose inception it was my privilege to have had a part.

It is well for this city to-day to pause a little in the bustle of its daily life, and with formal ceremony to lay the corner-stone of this building, which for generations is to be the centre of its municipal activity.

This is the one building that in the broadest, truest way always has reflected and always will the life of the city. The rich memories of the past, the life of the present, and the brightest hopes for the future, all cluster around it, and within its walls will find a full and true expression. Whatever is good and just and noble in our municipal life, together with its faults, its errors, and its shortcomings, will be the history written on its walls, by which posterity will judge how well we did the duty set before us. Because it

THE RINDGE GIFTS. 49

is and is to be an epitome of our city's history, we gather here to-day to ask the blessing of God upon this work, and upon our dear old city, to which again we pledge our love and loyalty.

This building marks the fourth distinct change in the home of our town government, and, speaking generally, each marks an epoch in the life of this community.

For nearly one hundred years after the town was founded the meeting-house was the town-house. That was distinctly the period of union of church and state. This union of home was the natural consequence of union of life. Only church members were voters. Once a month they were called together in the meeting-house " at the ringing of the bell," upon town business. There taxes were voted for the support of church and town, and the church was the most frequent and important subject of town action. The old chronicles constantly speak of ." the people of this church and towne." Truly "church and town were but the names for one and the same constituency. The town was the church acting in secular concerns, and the church was the town acting in religious concerns." Those were times of plain and simple life, when strong and God-fearing men in prayer and faith were laying deep the foundations upon which was to be built a great and prosperous community. To their earnest purpose, serious life, deep devotion, and unflinching faith may we never fail to acknowledge our great indebtedness. They were not seeking how easiest to live, but how best to live, "for God's glory and the church's good;" they were church building, nation building, establishing institutions to last as long as men fear God and love liberty. They made the church the life of the state, and around it they established the public school, the college, and the printing-press. Religion, education, self-government, — these were the corner-stones for an enduring structure, materials from which to make commonwealths that were to last.

The close union of church and town necessarily, in the growth of both, came to an end. There came the time for emancipation from church control, though not from church influence. The faith of the early founders was not forgotten nor neglected. In 1708 the town government left its old home in the meeting-house, and uniting with the county, erected a building to be used as a town house and court house. This new union lasted till 1832. This change, too, marked an epoch in the life of the town. It passes now from church government to self-government. It is distinctly the period of town-meeting. In that school of pure democracy our ancestors were taught those priceless lessons of equality, independence, and self-government which made them know their rights, and, knowing, dare maintain them. From the town-meeting sprang our independence and our republic.

Then came the third epoch in our town's history, as marked by a change in its public meetings. In 1832 the town, with a population of over six thousand, found its old quarters insufficient and inconvenient for its town-meetings. A bitter quarrel over Cambridge Common, which brought out over five hundred voters, had impressed this fact upon it. In this year (1832) it built its first distinctive town-house, changing the location from Old Cambridge to Cambridgeport. This, as town and city, it occupied till its destruction by fire in 1853, when it moved to the present City Hall. While this change is not exactly coincident with our change from a town to a city, yet, speaking roughly, it marks the period when a great growth in population, wealth, and town work made it necessary to discard old forms and institutions, and develop into full municipal life. It is distinctly the period of material prosperity.

THE RINDGE GIFTS.

The population of the town has increased from six thousand to nearly seventy thousand; its valuation from three to over sixty millions; industries unnumbered have been established in our midst; churches and schools have multiplied; and contentment and happiness, with God's blessing, seem to have rested upon our people. Nor have the lessons of its earlier life been forgotten. The prayers and faith of pious founders are still with us; the patriotism, independence, and equality taught in the old town-meeting have been an inspiration to this generation bravely to do its duty and give of its strength for union and liberty.

But what epoch will this new home, whose cornerstone we lay to-day, mark in our municipal life? It is early yet to say, but not too early to express a wish and a belief.

I verily believe and hope it marks a period of larger things, of a greater, grander municipal life, of a larger public spirit in works of philanthropy and charity, of a broadening out of our lives more into the lives of others, and of devotion to the charities that "soothe and heal and bless." All the signs portend the beginning of such a glorious era. There is inspiration for us in the work and life of him whose noble generosity and public spirit have so richly blessed this city.

In one of the many letters in which he shows his keen and constant interest in the public work he has here undertaken he says: "What I am aiming to do is to establish certain didactic public buildings." And so upon each he has written a lesson it is to teach. This building he wishes ever to remind us that the laws of men spring from God's commandments, that it is honorable faithfully to administer these laws, and upon their enforcement rests good government. But there is another lesson these buildings forever will teach, which his modesty forbids him to mention,—the lesson of a noble life and fortune devoted to God and to his fellow-men.

Surely under happy auspices, with an example before us of a pure, unselfish, Christian life, with public spirit and noble generosity, the corner-stone of our new City Hall is laid. God grant that it mark the beginning of the best and grandest period in the life of this old city!

REMARKS OF T. W. HIGGINSON.

We stand to-day beside the foundation of a building yet to be erected, — of a building which as yet exists only in the generous purpose of its donor, or in the carefully prepared plans and contracts in which his intention has thus far embodied itself. We meet, therefore, to celebrate a great public purpose rather than a completed fulfilment, — a man, rather than a building. As a citizen who has happened to be brought more closely in contact with Mr. Rindge than most of those here present, — although we have never met face to face, — I wish to speak of that aspect of the occasion which would interest him least, its relations to himself. It very often happens that the good which a man does seems half an accident; the gift seems greater and much more interesting than the man. It is indeed rather a drawback upon the modern American way of founding great institutions during one's life, instead of by one's last will and testament, that the donor himself sometimes remains as an encumbrance and an interference, and the community becomes a little impatient to pay tribute to all his services by an eloquent funeral inscription. He is petty or vain, he is captious or interfering. I wish to say that I have never encountered any public benefactor who was so totally the opposite of all these undesirable qualities as Mr. Rindge. If his whole correspondence with myself, and, I doubt not,

THE RINDGE GIFTS. 53

with all the members of the citizens' Committee, could be published verbatim, it would reveal as absolutely simple and straightforward a human being as I ever encountered. I cannot conceive of a man more entirely absorbed in doing good, or more free from self-consciousness in the process; nor can I imagine one more reasonable, more considerate than he, although engaged in the difficult position of carrying out his purposes through agents living at the other extremity of a continent. Startled, like the rest of you, by this sudden series of great public benefactions, I began with the fear that he from whom they came, and whom, as I said, I had never seen, might be a man of mere impulse or a man of whim. But I have seen him tested as to his purposes and methods in connection with the City Hall, the Public Library, and above all, the more difficult problem of the Manual Training School. I should say, as the result, that he is a man remarkable, not for public spirit alone, but for level-headed judgment and common-sense.

Now, as to the uses of a City Hall itself. Never having been myself a mayor, — and not, therefore, belonging to that uncrowned senate of ex-mayors whom we in Cambridge find so useful, — I have only learned enough about building city halls to discover the fact that we have a great many departments which need lodging in such a building, and that the head of each department thinks it very essential that his particular rooms should have a southern exposure, an easy approach, an ante-room, a private stairway, and a good set of arm-chairs. This is all as it should be. The enormous expansion of city life throughout Massachusetts is only what is going on in all civilized countries, and we must simply accept it. A modern self-governing city is merely the effort of fifty thousand or one hundred thousand people to secure for themselves and their posterity better houses, better streets, better lighting, better schools, better libraries, better parks than the richest of them could get without this organization. We all praise the simplicity of the old town-meeting days, but we all do our best to get beyond them as quickly as possible. I do not see how any one who has eyes in his head can help seeing that all this tendency is increasing, not diminishing. For one, I cannot in the least perceive why, if a city supplies us with water, it should not some day supply us with gas, as I cannot see why the nation which manages the post-office should not at some time manage the telegraph, and even the railroads themselves. But all this is for the future. Meanwhile let us accept the city for what it is, and work within its recognized limitations for the public good. The best return we can make to Mr. Rindge for the Manual Training School is to fill it with young students who will take a pride in it, as they do now, and will take a still greater pride when it comes to be connected in an indirect and modest way, as it will be next year, with our great University. The best return we can make for the new Public Library is to fill it with good books, through a citizens' subscription; and then to bring all parts of the city and all the public schools into contact with those books. The best return we can make for the new City Hall is to fill it with clean politics.

General EDWARD W. HINCKS was then called upon, and responded as follows:—

REMARKS BY GENERAL EDWARD W. HINCKS.

YOUR HONOR, GENTLEMEN OF THE CITY COUNCIL, FRATERS AND FELLOW-CITIZENS,— In compliance with the request of His Honor the Mayor, I rise to occupy a few moments; but as the time is so limited I shall not detain you with any extended remarks. The honors of this day justly belong to others, and especially to our friend, the past Mayor, who has

THE RINDGE GIFTS. 55

been so largely instrumental in accomplishing the purpose which has occasioned our gathering here.

It cannot but be a gratifying thought to all the citizens of Cambridge that one born and reared in their midst and educated at their public schools, who has gone out from among them and acquired broad and manly views of personal duty by observation of other scenes and association with other communities, should cherish such a grateful appreciation of the institutions of his native city, and such an affectionate regard for her character, scenes, and traditions, as to deem her worthy of the munificent gifts he has recently bestowed upon her, including this projected City Hall.

It is also a gratifying reflection to all who esteem the value of faithful administration, to the moral as well as to the material welfare of the community, that the mind of the donor is so deeply impressed with the importance of reminding the people that fidelity in the administration of public affairs is of the first consequence, that he has accompanied this magnificent gift with the condition that a precept, to the effect that "It is honorable and praiseworthy to faithfully serve the people by helping to administer the laws," with other inscriptions of similar import, shall be conspicuously and permanently maintained in metal or stone over the portals, where all who enter may see them, and thereby be continually reminded of their duty to the city and to their fellow-men. This is a most beneficent and valuable feature of this gift, teaching line upon line, precept upon precept, that he who enters here must be faithful to his trust.

May we not hope that this entire structure will be completed, in emulation of this virtue, with such faithfulness to contract and obligation that it will of itself be a constant and permanent lesson of integrity and honor; and that as exemplified in the work of laying the chief stone of the corner which we have witnessed to-day, every part, to the last lintel, architrave, and cornice, to the topmost pinnacle, finial, or spire, will be executed with such fidelity to design and specification, with such mechanical skill and perfection, so level and square, that all will unite with one voice and pronounce it good and true.

And, when completed, let it always be a temple of honor, where intrigue and corruption shall not enter, and whose occupants shall be faithful servants of the people, honestly administering their affairs on business principles, and holding public office as a sacred public trust, impartially executing the laws for the preservation of good order and the promotion of public morality, sobriety, and virtue, so that the people may never mourn because the wicked rule, but ever rejoice because the righteous bear sway and fearlessly represent the principles and purposes cherished by our fathers who erected their homes where they could enjoy religious freedom and intellectual independence, here in the wilderness, which has been transformed into a great city, the seat of learning, the abode of industry, and the home of contentment, and yet retains the freedom and independence our fathers sought.

By such a consummation of the wishes of the donor and the desires of our citizens who fully appreciate them, Cambridge will be doubly blessed by precept and example, constantly stimulating her people to the greatest effort to attain good government and to cultivate principles for the advancement of the moral, social, and material welfare of the community, which cannot but have a beneficent influence in forming the character of those who are to succeed to the duties and responsibilities which must soon pass from the control of the present generation, but which we reverently trust will ever be faithfully borne by a people whose God is the Lord.

THE RINDGE GIFTS. 57

Mayor HART of Boston was introduced as the next speaker; but he was very brief, simply saying that he had brought the congratulations of the city of Boston to her sister city, Cambridge, and whatever redounds to Cambridge redounds to Boston.

Grand Marshal GEORGE H. RHODES then made the customary proclamation that the stone had been properly laid, and Grand Chaplain SKINNER pronounced the benediction. During the ceremonies the quartet sang several selections, and the band played appropriate pieces.

The exercises on the transfer of the new City Hall to the City Government took place on the evening of Dec. 9, 1890, and were, by desire of Mr. Rindge, very simple in character, the attendance being also confined to those who could be accommodated in the aldermen's room.

At half-past seven the invited guests made their appearance at the door, and were given seats behind the railing that divides the members' seats from the rest of the room. A little later the aldermen filed in, taking their seats at the new desks. They were soon followed by members of the Common Council, who took their seats, as in joint convention, just behind the aldermen. At eight o'clock Mayor H. H. Gilmore, with Col. Francis J. Parker, the legal representative of Mr. Rindge, and Rev. Dr. Francis G. Peabody, of Harvard College, took their seats on the mayor's platform. Colonel Parker sat on the right of the Mayor, and Rev. Dr. Peabody on his left. In front and on one side near the mayor's platform were the special guests of the city, among whom were Governor-elect William E. Russell, Col. T. W. Higginson, Rev. Lucius R. Paige, the first city clerk, and historian of Cambridge, President Charles W. Eliot, of Harvard College, ex-mayors Henry O. Houghton, Charles H. Saunders, James M. W. Hall, Frank A. Allen, Samuel L. Montague, and James A. Fox. Hon. A. B. Alger, mayor-elect, was detained away by a previous engagement. There were present also many of the members' wives and other ladies, while the gallery near the top of the chamber was crowded to its full capacity. The Oxford quartet opened the exercises by a vocal selection, after which Mayor H. H. GILMORE, who presided, arose and asked all to join Rev. F. G. PEABODY in prayer, who prayed that God's blessing might rest on the new building and the people who should have charge of the city's affairs, and that the fear of the Lord might govern the men who should rule there. The prayer was followed by a song from the quartet, and then Mayor Gilmore introduced Mr. Rindge's representative, Colonel FRANCIS J. PARKER, who spoke as follows: —

REMARKS BY COLONEL PARKER.

YOUR HONOR AND GENTLEMEN, — I feared that in representing our friend to-night I should fail something in what was due him and yourselves. I want to congratulate you and your people on your accession to your pleasant present quarters, and I am glad to be present at your house-warming. I trust you may find the city's routine of business run more smoothly in your new City Hall. I think the city engineer will perhaps find his work facilitated, especially in drains. I think the city messenger will find greater speed in his increased facilities, and have no doubt the city clerk will experience new sensations in the ease with which he will hereafter make records of marriages and marriage intentions; and, Colonel Higginson, you must allow me to thank you and your Committee for the devotion you have shown in attention to every detail until the completion of this building. I am sorry Mr. Rindge could not be here to convey his personal thanks for the appreciative manner in which the gift has been received. I am sure he will be glad when he hears from me of the interest taken by his former fellow-citizens in the new building.

Colonel Parker then handed the deed, in roll form, tied with a red, white, and blue ribbon, to Colonel Higginson, the representative of the Citizens' Committee on Rindge Gifts, who said: —

REMARKS OF COLONEL HIGGINSON.

I cannot receive this deed in behalf of the Citizens' Committee on Rindge Gifts without taking occasion to say a few words of our benefactor's representative, Colonel Parker, — how much his direct co-operation has assisted the Committee ; how much their labors have been lightened by his co-operation. The responsibility itself in all respects has not always been agreeable. The processes of expenditure have sometimes been embarrassing, but we have always fallen back upon Mr. Parker. He has drawn all the checks, and has given some of them, — he has toned down, that is, our sometimes rather vague and ambitious desires. We have sometimes done things by his advice which we should not have thought of. He has protected us from the architects ; and to be able to master these pleasing despots is the effort of a life-time.

Turning to the Mayor, he said, —

This deed represents the last of the series of great benefactions, and I desire to unroll it, first to show it to you, and then to the citizens, in order that you may see what a *bona fide* document it is, lacking nothing to express that noble and generous — exceptionally generous — heart, though it might indeed be more characteristic of the giver if the seal in the corner were heart-shaped instead of the regulation seal. To us from the beginning, Mr. Rindge has been the same high-minded, good-natured benefactor, and we have never had occasion to urge him to do more than his own kind nature has prompted him to do. In our city we are still in that stage of progress in which the Greek states were, at a very early period, when only the public buildings were large and costly, and the private houses comparatively modest. Thus among us, if you see a brick or stone building, it is usually for a city hall, or a church, or a schoolhouse, or to shelter a chemical engine or the city horses; while we and our children dwell in houses made only of wood. This is fitting, that we should think more of the city than of ourselves; and we may hope that the city affairs will be better administered because of the dignity and beauty of this their dwelling.

I have heard that while in Boston Mr. Rindge asked his physician to be allowed only one half hour in which to visit this city, — and especially to visit the Manual Training School; and when it was found he could not come, the superintendent sent one of the boys over to talk to Mr. Rindge, who took much interest in examining his proficiency and hearing the details of the school. His inability even to look upon the buildings he has erected and the institutions he founded must have been among the great disappointments of his life, and we share the disappointment.

In closing, Mr. Mayor, I transfer to you, as representative of the city, this valuable document, and am glad to be able to express the opinion, founded on much official as well as personal intercourse, that you can be succeeded in coming years by no mayor whose record will be more upright and stainless than your own.

The deed of gift being then handed to the Mayor, he replied as follows: —

MAYOR GILMORE'S SPEECH.

Cambridge is proud to-day, not alone because she is placed in possession of this building, but, as well, because one of her worthy sons, moved by the generous impulses of a great heart, has given it to her.

Were this solely to measure the limits of Mr. Rindge's well-considered liberality in giving to the city of his nativity, he would still be distinguished among the comparatively few men who have made great public donations. When, therefore, to this gift you add the new Public Library building and the park upon which it is located, and upon which the new English High School-house is being erected by the city, you reach an aggregate of public benefactions seldom paralleled.

It is, sir, my happy privilege for and in behalf of the city of Cambridge to receive and accept the gift of this building, through your hands, as the representative of Mr. Frederick H. Rindge.

Let me beg of you to convey to him the high sense of his generosity entertained by the people of Cambridge; their profound thanks for this latest and grandest gift; their sincere regrets at his enforced absence on this occasion; with their heart-warm prayers for his happiness and the prolonged enjoyment of a life devoted, as his is, to the promotion of all that stands for truth, purity, and justice. Assure him also of the pleasure experienced in welcoming to Cambridge, for the second time, his trusty friend and adviser, Col. Francis J. Parker, as I now do most heartily. Do not allow your well-known modesty, my dear sir, to compel you to withhold from him the fact that the felicity of this occasion was enhanced by the unapproachable service performed in his behalf.

It may be interesting to review, somewhat, the past history of Cambridge, and compare its present extent, wealth, development, and financial status with certain of its earlier periods. Little less than two hundred and fifty years ago the town of Cambridge, which may justly be called the mother of towns, was about thirty-six miles in length, extending from Dedham to the Merrimac River, with an area covering more than seventy square miles. Within its boundaries were the city of Newton, the Brighton district of Boston, the towns of Arlington, Lexington, Bedford, and Billerica. To-day the area is reduced to $5\frac{449}{1000}$ square miles. One hundred years ago the population was about two thousand five hundred, and the valuation of all property slightly exceeded £59,000, or $295,000.00, yielding to each person one hundred and eighteen dollars on the average. To meet the general expenses, taxes were laid of one penny in the pound, — equal to forty cents on each one hundred dollars. To-day, with a population of seventy thousand, and a valuation of nearly seventy millions, equivalent to about $1000 for each inhabitant, the general appropriations are over two millions of dollars, at a tax rate of $1.56 per $100. Then the people were living in the strictest simplicity. Any steady and industrious laboring man may live to-day in the enjoyment of home comforts and conveniences then beyond the reach of the most opulent. There was no common water supply, no fire department,

THE RINDGE GIFTS. 63

no police department, no street-lighting; nor were there edge-stones or bricked sidewalks, no paved or macadamized streets, no common sewers, no salaried officials; there was no bonded debt. The schoolhouses and public buildings were of a primitive character, and school-teachers' salaries less than $300; though they were required to teach both Latin and English, and be accomplished to write and cipher. The salaries of the five schoolmasters in 1833 were for each $550. A moderate compensation for actual time given was paid to school-committee men one hundred years ago; yet the selectmen, one of whom served as town clerk, performed gratuitous service, but they had occasional entertainment at the public house at public expense.

Even sixty years ago, with a population of six thousand five hundred, and a property valuation of $3,000,000, a tax rate of $22\frac{6}{10}$ cents on $100 furnished the necessary revenue of $8,400 to defray current annual expenses. The State tax was $8.57. Fifty years ago the tax rate was only $27\frac{7}{10}$ cents per $100. The population had gained to eight thousand five hundred. The State tax was $14.29. The town debt was $40,000, and the valuation nearly $4,500,000. Jan. 1, 1890, the entire municipal bonded indebtedness, less sinking-fund assets, was $2,333,333; the valuation $65,250,000, with a State tax of not far from $60,000.

When the town became a city, in 1846, the public debt was reduced to $22,000; valuation under $10,000,000. In 1866, $870,000 was the amount of the city debt. The valuation had been increased to $28,000,000. In 1876 the net debt was something in excess of $4,000,000; valuation $66,750,000, — an increase of twenty millions in five years; instances of remarkable inflation. That the valuations were inordinate, witness the reduction of nearly $17,000,000 in the two following years. High-water mark had been reached both in valuation and indebtedness.

Within fifteen years the public debt has been largely reduced, notwithstanding the enormous expenditures occasioned by the remarkable growth and development manifest in every section of the city during this period, and never more noticeable than during the last four years.

The first ascertained assessment for construction of a main drain was in 1845. It was located in Ward 2, and cost $958. The amount of expenditures for sewers in 1847 was $13; in 1874 it was nearly $259,000. The appropriation for 1890 was $65,000.

The seat of government of town and city has been several times changed, and each removal has appeared to mark the beginning of a new epoch. Let us take courage; the future is full of promise.

In the early days, and until about 1708, town-meetings were held in the meeting-house in Harvard Square; later, in the building erected for use of the town and the county court, in the same locality. The town in 1756 agreed to share the expense in erecting a new court and town house, which was used until 1832. March 5, 1832, the town meeting was held in the new town house, built on Harvard Street, corner of Norfolk, at a cost of $4351.09 for construction, furnishing, and fencing the lot.

The meeting of the first City Council was held in that building, and meetings were there continued until December 29, 1853, when fire destroyed the edifice, which was insured for $2,000.

Subsequently, until this day, the City Hall, corner of Main and Pleasant Streets, has been the seat of government.

Between the years 1850 and 1860 several undertakings of great importance to the growing city were entered upon or consummated. The Fresh Pond water supply was secured. The purchase was made of thirty-two acres of land, and the erection thereon of the present almshouse, at

THE RINDGE GIFTS. 65

a gross cost of $48,000. Land was purchased for the Cambridge Cemetery. The West Boston and Canal bridges became free public avenues forever. Later followed the filling of the low-land districts.

Between 1880 and 1890 was secured the annexation of the Belmont district; the Commonwealth granted to Cambridge all riparian rights to the borders of Fresh Pond, to secure the purity of its waters, — an act then without precedent in the history of the State; the Stony Brook auxiliary water supply was secured; the new Harvard bridge and avenue were built; and the munificent public donations made to the city by Mr. Frederick H. Rindge.

Standing here, then, after the lapse of two hundred and sixty years, where the few unimportant and straggling habitations of our hardy, pious, and ever-to-be-revered ancestors were first established; contemplating their efforts, their sacrifices, their steadfast devotion to the principles of civil and religious liberty; and recognizing their invaluable help in establishing an independent and republican form of government, — with the door to progress wide open before us, let us resolve that we will continue inflexibly true to the sentiments with which they were animated, to the end that however great and powerful, wealthy and important, this city may become as the years roll on, it still can be the pride and boast of her people that she is honestly and discreetly governed, for the best interests of all, without partiality or discrimination.

TRANSFER TO THE COMMITTEE.

His Honor then turned to the Chairman of the Committee on Public Property and said: —

ALDERMAN FRASIER, — To the important Committee on Public Property, of which you are the chairman, is now intrusted the custody, care, and repairs of this grand building, with all its adornments and modern equipments. The zeal and energy displayed by every member of your efficient Committee during the past year, and especially in relation to furnishing and preparing these premises for the occupancy and convenient use of the several departments of the government, deserve high commendation; and this, in connection with your many years of faithful public service, renders the formal act of placing this property in your charge one of great pleasure and satisfaction.

CHAIRMAN FRASIER'S RESPONSE.

MR. MAYOR, — It gives me great pleasure, on behalf of the Committee on Public Property, to receive the custody of this great building, the gift of a noble and generous son of Cambridge, and one that every citizen may well feel proud of; but we regret very much that we are deprived of his presence on this occasion. Since it has become the duty of the Committee to furnish this building it has been our aim to do it in a manner that would compare favorably with the building and meet with the approval of Mr. Rindge; and we thank the City Council for the assistance rendered us without a single dictation, and we hope that it will meet with their approval also. It has been our endeavor to please all, and if we have failed, it is no fault of ours; and considering the short time it is to remain in our charge, we hope to be able to surrender it to our successors with as much credit as we now receive it. Your Honor, I thank you for the kind words you have conveyed to me, and the Committee will, I have no doubt, greatly appreciate them.

With a selection by the quartet the exercises closed.

MAIN ENTRANCE, CITY HALL

DESCRIPTION
OF
THE CITY HALL BUILDING.

THE Cambridge City Hall occupies the end of a block on Main Street, with an open street on either side. Standing well back and above Main Street, upon terraces and walls necessitated by the slope of the ground, its simple dignity is seen to good advantage, and its tower is visible for miles around. The front, a hundred and fifty-seven feet long, and facing the south, is given up to offices; while the rear is used principally for the rooms used at night by the City Council.

The building is ninety-two feet deep on the sides, but has a recessed court thirty-two by thirty-seven feet at the back, which is a principal feature of its plan.

In general form the building is Mediæval, but carried out in a spirit of free Romanesque, which allows its broad wall surfaces, built of quarry face-stone, and its construction and openings to be emphasized and made interesting by simply ornamenting the structural members, rather than by constructing ornamental members, — which is the strength of the style, economically considered.

Long Meadow brown-stone has been used with the Milford granite, as an economical way of emphasizing the design and giving more detail and interest to the mass by contrast in color.

The front wall is broken only by the tower, twenty-seven feet square, which, rising a hundred and fifty-four feet from its terraced base, gives a commanding dignity and distinction to the building, and centres the interest and marks the principal entrance, which pierces its base. The tower, with open belfry, bell, and clock, marks the building as the centre of civic power and life, and has its prototype in the town-halls of the Netherlands, though unlike them in detail. The interest is still further centred in the entrance by the steps, platform, and lanterns, and by the balcony above, which also recalls the town-halls of Europe. This balcony, though suppressed in form and not needed for proclamations, as in Mediæval days, adds a point of interest. Here its front has been utilized by the architects as the most appropriate and conspicuous space for the inscription and lesson which Mr. Rindge wished to be placed on the front of the building.

On each side of the tower the walls are pierced by three tiers of windows, above the ample basement windows cut in the batter of the base courses.

The main story has transom windows directly under the round arched windows of the second story.

The low third-story windows, which light the less important rooms, rest on the bright crocketed string course which runs round the building and gives the effect of a frieze or attic story. They are enriched

THE RINDGE GIFTS.

with colonnettes, and with the sturdy corbelled cornice directly above their lintel course hold the general design together and top out the stone work in a spirited and effective way and give quiet value to the slate roof. From the attic story four of the windows are carried up with tall angle shafts into high gabled dormers, which light the roof space and enliven the design with broad masses of light and shade. By breaking the monotony of the roof and leading the eye up, they make the transition to the high tower less abrupt.

Great breadth has been given the design by accentuating the horizontal lines by means of brown-stone string courses and bands, and by the general color treatment.

Particular attention has been given to preserving plain wall-spaces where possible, and a source of strength has been gained by using the light granite for the angles. This is particularly noticeable in the tower, which gains in effective strength and height from the fact that the shaft rises unbroken from the terrace at its base to the belfry. The window-groups and clock increase this effect.

In the belfry story the upward shoot of the tower is increased above the flatly corbelled string course by the firm angle shafts of granite, while the open arcades and shafts and the rich crocketed capitals and the cornice, all of brown-stone, concentrate the interest and enrich the design. A feeling of openness and lightness is also gained, which prevents the massive tower from seeming heavy, and brings it into harmony with the arches and dormers below.

The effect of the tower has been still further lightened, and strengthened too, by slightly battering the walls and setting the belfry stage inside the lines of the tower below and continuing the slight taper. The tower is one hundred and twenty feet in height to the top of the stone cornice, and one hundred and fifty-four to the top of the finial, and contains a clock of the E. Howard Watch & Clock Company's manufacture, with a face on each of the four sides of the tower. The bell which strikes the hours is located just above the clock; it was cast by Messrs. Meneely & Co., of West Troy, N. Y., and weighs four thousand and forty-seven pounds. The following inscription is cast in raised letters upon the bell, —

> Cheerfully I ring the hour
> From my home within the tower;
> But I would a lesson teach, —
> Even bells men's hearts may reach.

> THE LESSON.
> Keep the ballot free and pure, —
> Thus the rights of all secure;
> Public wrong finds antidote
> When each voter casts his vote.

The finial, the bell-deck, gutters, conductors, cresting and all the flashing of the building are of copper.

As in the belfry, the attic story above the main string course has been set in a few inches, to give firmness and refinement to the design. Refinement has been given also, and a feeling of quiet horizontal movement, by changing the broad stone courses of

THE RINDGE GIFTS. 71

the first story and basement into alternating narrow and wide courses in the second and third stories.

In the rear the deep court-yard with walls and terraces, the drive-way sloping to the basement entrances on the court, and the blank walls at the ends of the assembly rooms, with frieze windows only, lend themselves to a more picturesque treatment, the result of practical requirements.

The court as designed brings the light and air well into the heart of the building, as well as lighting the offices, coat-rooms, and basement-rooms which open on to it. It also suggests the means of future enlargement, without destroying the present rooms, by making coat-rooms into corridors.

The basement opens directly on the level of the court, and is high and airy. Here are the workrooms of the Water-Board, the Superintendent of Lamps, and the heating and ventilating apparatus, which is worked by the Blower system. The air is taken in at the bell-deck of the tower, then heated and sent through the building by means of a fan, thus preventing over-heated pipes and air, and making a constant change of air.

Steps and terraces lead up to the rear entrances on the main floor from the two side streets.

Entering the building from Main Street, a broad walk and steps of blue-stone bring you to the open platform of the same material, with low walls and coping of brown-stone. The round-arched doorway is ornamented with a firm rich bead, and columns with carved caps and abaci, the lines of which continue across as a transom. Above this, the arch is glazed with a wrought-iron grille, on which the coat of arms of the city is wrought. The walls of the vestibule are of face brick with marble panels. The floor is of marble mosaic, with stone steps leading to the hall. At this point a wooden screen, with leaded glass, separates the vestibule from the hall directly opposite the staircase. Inside, a passage-way connects the City Clerk's and Auditors' Offices under the thick walls of the tower, and gives a treatment of great piers and brick arches which mark the tower and vaults above, and give a strong sense of carrying power and architectural strength.

A corridor, twelve feet wide, connects the two sides of the building and the elevator and staircase with the entrance. On the right a large space in addition to the corridor is added to accommodate the mass of persons assembled at certain seasons around the Auditors', Treasurers', and the Water-Board Offices. At this point is the Janitor's room and the corridor leading to the rear entrance on the right. On the left, at end of main corridor, is the City Messenger's Office, with its conspicuous leaded glass screen. On the front are offices used by the Mayor for general business. The rear corridor on this side gives access from the street and the building to the offices of the Street Department and School Department, — a group that can be cut off from the rest of the building if desired. The Street Department has a record vault, while across the building a large and small vault serve the purposes of the Treasurer and the Water-Board. The thick granite walls of the tower are utilized in the construction of the vaults of City Clerk and Auditor. These vaults are carried up into the story above and utilized by the Assessors and the Clerk of Committees; while the space between on the floor, lighted by three windows, forms a large office occupied by the Superintendent of Public Buildings, the Inspector of Buildings, and the Inspector of Wires. The staircase cage extends from the basement to the third story ceiling. The principal entrance to the basement is between the two staircases which run to a landing and then to the main floor. The staircase is composed of three runs around an open well on either side of the broad central flight which separates at a landing, runs right and left to a secondary landing, and reaches the floors above in two runs. This arrangement, with broad windows in front of each run, and the two open wells reaching from basement to third story, gives excellent lighting and air to each story and forms a handsome staircase, which is finished and wainscoted in oak like the high wainscoting of the halls, the doors, and the door and window finish of the building.

The piers supporting the floors and beams spanning the entrance to the staircase cage are of iron encased in moulded plaster with rich Romanesque capitals. This treatment has been followed in the principal halls, the Treasurer's Office, and other rooms where columns were needed in construction. In the third story the ceiling is finished with oak beams and plaster panels. The columns and brackets under the carrying beam are handsomely finished in oak, in keeping with the firm balusters and arched strings which carry the rail, and the staircase cage is consistently ended and brought into harmony with the rest of the woodwork.

Throughout the rest of the building the beams and modillion cornices are treated in plaster and painted in light ivory colors, to increase the effect of light and airiness, particularly in corridors.

The second story hall, running from the Mayor's Reception Room to the Committee Room on left and the principal Lavatory, gives easy access to the Assembly Rooms in the rear and to the offices on the front of the building. These are the offices of the Assessors with large vault over vault below, the Clerk of Committees with small vault, and the Superintendent of Buildings. The Mayor's private office has a southeast exposure on this corner and opens directly from the Reception Room, which is panelled to the shelf of the carved mantelpiece. The Aldermen's room, entered directly from the hall or from its antechamber, occupies two stories, with a coved ceiling running up into the roof. It is lighted on one side by high windows, which run into the broad frieze, and with pilasters form part of the decoration. Below the coving a rich modillion cornice breaks the height of the walls. On the side opposite the windows the cornice is carried on decorated columns and the space over the antechamber is utilized for a gallery for the public. Above the wainscoting of panelled oak, the broad wall space is treated in dull red on a rough leathery "texture" with "all over" design of light color glazed to a soft tone, in keeping with the ivory white tones of the cornice and ceiling mouldings and the warm browns and green of the frieze, which is divided into panels to correspond with the columns and pilaster treatment. The coving and the background of the coffered ceiling is treated in soft blue green tones. The ornament and some lines have been picked out in gold, giving refinement and sparkle to the effect, without destroying its quiet dignity.

Against the blank wall is the Mayor's desk, on a raised platform, with the Clerk in front and the desks and chairs of the Board ranged round in a semicircle inside the curved rail. All the furniture, benches, etc., are made from special designs, in keeping with the room, as is the fixed furniture for offices.

The Common Council Chamber, though smaller than the Aldermanic Chamber, is treated in a similar manner architecturally, but the walls are dull green, with lighter design glazed on, and the other colors treated in harmony. The rest of the decoration of the building is in tones of ivory and yellow, changing into a leathery brown, except the walls of the lower hall, which are of a soft red color above the wainscot line.

In the third story the wide corridor, over the corridor below, connects the double Committee-room on the southeast corner with the large Committee and Fire Department room on the west end. Next this on the corner is the suite of the City Engineer. The large Draughting-room is finished into the roof, and receives top light from a skylight. The Engineer's Private Office, and Library, also used for a committee-room, connect with the vault, which is fire-proof, lined with hollow walls of brick, and with a brick floor and ceiling carried on iron beams and iron shutters to the windows. This room occupies an entire story in the tower, and forms a safe repository for the valuable drawings and data belonging to the office. The rest of the rooms on the front of the building are used by the Board of Health and Inspector of Milk, with a common Laboratory between. In the rear, the space is occupied by the top of the Aldermen's Chamber and gallery, the top of the Council Chamber, and a large store-room. Over the closets in the Engineer's Room the stairs go up to the roof, which is also reached by the elevator.

The building has brick firestops wherever practicable, and all the principal partitions are of brick carried up to or through the attic.

In the attic, or roof story, are store-rooms, light shafts, and the great air-duct, which carries fresh air from the open belfry stage to the heating chamber.

The roof is carried on the brick walls which run up through the attic, and on the roof girders which rest upon the main and partition walls below.

NOTE.

THE Citizens' Committees appointed by the City Council, at the suggestion of Mr. RINDGE, to take charge of the erection of the Public Library and the City Hall were regarded as discharged from office on the completion of these buildings. It was the desire of Mr. Rindge, however, that the Committee which originally had charge of the erection of the Manual Training School should remain as the "Supervisory Committee" of the institution until such time as it should be transferred to the city. As this transfer has never yet taken place, — Mr. Rindge having assumed, for an indefinite period, the expenses of the school, — this Committee is still in office, but has added to its numbers, at different times, as follows, with the approval of Mr. Rindge.

Mr. WILLIAM B. CABOT was appointed on the Supervisory Committee of the Manual Training School on the 10th of February, 1890, and resigned March 1, 1891.

Prof. WINFIELD S. CHAPLIN and Hon. HENRY H. GILMORE were appointed on the Committee on the 13th day of January, 1891.

The following list of Committees should also be preserved : —

COMMITTEES OF THE SCHOOL COMMITTEE ON THE MANUAL TRAINING SCHOOL.

May, 1888.

John L. Hildreth, M. D.   Hon. William H. Orcutt.

June, 1890.

Hon. Asa P. Morse.   Prof. Winfield S. Chaplin.

SPECIAL COMMITTEES OF THE CITY COUNCIL ON THE RINDGE GIFTS.

1887.

Aldermen DANIEL E. FRASIER and CHARLES F. STRATTON. *Councilmen* ALVIN F. SORTWELL, JAMES H. MCPECK, and FRANKLIN W. HAYNES.

1888.

His Honor Mayor RUSSELL and *Aldermen* DANIEL E. FRASIER and CHARLES F. STRATTON. President ALVIN F. SORTWELL and *Councilmen* JAMES H. MCPECK, FRANKLIN W. HAYNES, and WILLIAM T. PIPER.

1889.

His Honor Mayor GILMORE and *Aldermen* DANIEL E. FRASIER and GUSTAVUS GOEPPER. President EDWARD A. BINGHAM and *Councilmen* DANIEL F. KENNEDY, PATRICK J. LAMBERT, and JOHN T. PHELAN.

1890.

His Honor Mayor GILMORE and *Aldermen* DANIEL E. FRASIER and JOHN R. FAIRBAIRN. President EDWARD A. BINGHAM and *Councilmen* J. HENRY RUSSELL, MARSHALL N. STEARNS, and CHARLES W. CHENEY.

www.ingramcontent.com/pod-product-compliance
Lightning Source LLC
Chambersburg PA
CBHW021949160426
43195CB00011B/1295